C# 12 Essentials A Comprehensive Guide

From the basics to advanced techniques of C# 12 development

Ziggy Rafiq

Website:	https://ziggyrafiq.com
LinkedIn:	https://www.linkedin.com/in/ziggyrafiq/
GitHub:	https://github.com/ziggyrafiq
Instagram	https://www.instagram.com/ziggyrafiq/
Facebook	https://www.facebook.com/ziggyrafiq
Twitter/X	https://twitter.com/ziggyrafiq

Copyright © 2024 Ziggy Rafiq

All rights reserved.

ISBN: 9798328661478

DEDICATION

A tribute to Ziggy Rafiq's late mother, Mrs. Zubeda Begum, this book is dedicated to her unwavering love, support, and encouragement. Ziggy's journey was profoundly shaped by her presence in his life from January 1st, 1950, until December 1st, 2022. It is a tribute to her enduring legacy that inspired this book.

SPECIAL THANKS

FAMILY AND FRIENDS: Ziggy would like to extend his deepest gratitude to his wife, children, and father, Mohammed Rafiq, for their support, patience, and understanding throughout the writing process.

MENTORS AND ADVISERS: Thanks to Ziggy's mentors and advisers for their guidance and valuable insights, enriching this book.

THE SOFTWARE ENGINEER COMMUNITY: Thank you to the vibrant online community of software engineers for sharing knowledge and providing inspiration.

MRS ZUBEDA BEGUM(LATE): Ziggy Rafiq continues to be inspired daily by the legacy of love and encouragement she left behind.

ABOUT THE AUTHOR

BACKGROUND AND EXPERTISE

With over 19 years of experience, Ziggy Rafiq has demonstrated exceptional skills in System Architecture. He has been a full-stack designer and developer for over 19 years. As a Technical Lead Developer in 2004, he demonstrated his leadership and expertise.

It was Ziggy Rafiq's groundbreaking work in 2002 that earned him the Shell Award after he developed an impenetrable login system. At the Microsoft Hero Event in 2008, he was named one of Microsoft's Top 10 Developers in the West Midlands.

Ziggy Rafiq has been recognized as an MVP, VIP, and Member of the Month by C# Corner (March 2024, July 2023), as well as an active speaker and Chapter Lead at the UK Developer Community.

EDUCATIONAL BACKGROUND

As a student at college, Ziggy Rafiq earned an American Associate Degree in Interactive Multimedia Communication. He obtained a BA Hons in Interactive Multimedia Communication 2:1 from the University of Wolverhampton between 1999 and 2003. Along the way, he acquired a comprehensive understanding of Design, Development, Testing, Deployment, and Project Management, which allowed him to be an effective professional.

Table of Contents

Chapter 1: Introduction to C# 12
Purpose of the Book 12
Scope of the Book 12
- Essential Concepts 12
- Object-Oriented Programming (OOP) 12
- Web Development with C# 12
- Advanced Topics 12
- Best Practices and Tips 12

What to Expect 12
Let's Get Started 13
Brief History of the C# Programming Language 13
- Key Milestones 13
- Impact and Significance 13

Overview of the C# Programming Language 13
- Key Features 13

Advantages of C# 14
- Simplicity 14
- Scalability 14
- Rich Features 14

Importance of Mastering C# for Both Beginners and Experts 14
- For Beginners 14
- For Experts 14

Importance and Relevance in Modern Software Development 14
- Widely Used Across Domains 14

Integration with the .NET Framework 15
- Robust Ecosystem 15
- Platform Independence 15

New Features and Enhancements in C# 12 15
- Continuous Improvement 15

Improved Productivity 15

Chapter 2: Getting Started with C# 16

Setting up the Development Environment 16

Introduction 16

Required Tools 16

Step-by-Step Guide 16

Basic Syntax and Structure of C# Programs 16

Introduction 16

Control Flow Statements 16

Writing and Running Your First C# Program 16

Step-by-Step Guide 16

"Hello World" Program 16

Understanding Basic Syntax and Structure 17

In-depth Explanation 17

Access Modifiers 17

Constructors, Properties, and Methods 17

Chapter 3: Data Types and Variables 18

Primitive Data Types 18

Declaring and Initializing Variables 18

Type Conversion and Casting 19

Importance of Understanding Data Types and Variables 19

Best Practices for Working with Data Types and Variables 19

Chapter 4: Operators and Expressions 20

Arithmetic, Relational, Logical, and Bitwise Operators 20

Arithmetic Operators 20

Relational Operators 21

Logical Operators 21

Bitwise Operators 22

Precedence and Associativity Rules 22

Console.WriteLine($"The result is {result}"); 23

Using Expressions in C# Programs 23

Importance of Understanding Operators and Expressions 23

Best Practices for Working with Operators and Expressions 23

Chapter 5: Control Flow and Decision-Making 25

Conditional Statements (if, else, switch) 25

    if Statement 25

    else Statement 25

    switch Statement 26

Looping Structures (for, while, do-while) 26

    for Loop 26

    while Loop 26

    do-while Loop 27

Branching and Control Flow Mechanisms 27

Importance of Understanding Control Flow and Decision-Making 27

Best Practices for Working with Control Flow and Decision-Making 28

Chapter 6: Arrays and Collections 29

Arrays: Single-Dimensional, Multi-Dimensional 29

    Single-Dimensional Arrays 29

    Multi-Dimensional Arrays 29

Console.WriteLine(matrix[0, 0]); 29

Lists, Dictionaries, and Other Collection Types 30

    Lists 30

    Dictionaries 30

Working with Collections: Iteration, Manipulation, Sorting 30

Declaring and Initializing Arrays 31

Working with Multidimensional Arrays 31

Introduction to Collections 32

Chapter 7: Methods and Functions 34

Declaring and Calling Methods 34

Passing Parameters: Value vs. Reference 35

Returning Values from Methods 36

Handling Method Overloading 36

- Importance of Methods and Functions 37
- Best Practices for Working with Methods and Functions 37

Chapter 8: Object-Oriented Programming (OOP) Basics 38
- Classes and Objects 38
- Encapsulation, Inheritance, Polymorphism 39
- Constructors and Destructors 41
- Access Modifiers and Visibility 42
- Importance of OOP Principles 42
- Best Practices for Implementing OOP Concepts 42

Chapter 9: Exception Handling 43
- Handling Exceptions Using try-catch Blocks 43
- Throwing and Catching Exceptions 43
- Handling and Throwing Exceptions in C# 44
- try-catch-finally Blocks 44
- Custom Exception Classes 45
- Best Practices for Exception Handling 46

Chapter 10: File I/O and Serialization 47
- Reading from and Writing to Files 47
- Working with Streams and Readers/Writers 48
- Serialization and Deserialization of Objects 48
- Handling Exceptions in File I/O Operations 50
- Best Practices for File I/O and Serialization 50

Chapter 11: Introduction to Asynchronous Programming 51
- Understanding Asynchronous and Synchronous Operations 51
- Using async and await Keywords 52
- Handling Asynchronous Exceptions 53
- Asynchronous Programming with async/await 55
- Best Practices for Asynchronous Programming 56

Chapter 12: Working with Databases 57
- Connecting to Databases using ADO.NET 57
- Executing SQL Queries and Commands 58

Working with Datasets and Data Readers 59

Handling Exceptions in Database Operations 60

Best Practices for Working with Databases 60

Chapter 13: Advanced Topics 61

Abstract Classes and Interfaces 61

Abstract Classes 61

Interfaces 62

Method Overriding and Virtual Methods 62

Access Modifiers and Class Members 63

Delegates and Events 64

Generics and Collections 64

LINQ (Language Integrated Query) 65

Lambda Expressions and LINQ 65

Attributes and Reflection 65

Wrapping Up Advanced Topics 65

Chapter 14: C# 12 Features 66

Overview of New Features in C# 12 66

Pattern Matching Enhancements 66

Record Types 67

Switch Expressions 67

Examples and Practical Usage 68

Simplifying Code with Records 68

Expressive Switch Expressions 68

Best Practices for Adoption 68

Future Trends and Advancements 68

Chapter 15: Best Practices and Tips 69

Coding Standards and Conventions 69

Naming Conventions 69

Formatting Rules 69

Commenting Practices 70

Performance Optimization Techniques 70

- Algorithm Optimization 70
- Data Caching 70
- Asynchronous Programming 70
- Visual Studio Debugging Tools 70
- Diagnosing Common Issues 70
- Writing Clean and Maintainable Code 70
  - Code Readability 70
  - Modularity 70
- Documentation and Commenting 70
  - Comments for Clarity 71
  - XML Documentation 71
- Continuous Improvement and Learning 71
  - Stay Updated 71
  - Embrace Lifelong Learning 71
  - Apply What You Learn 71
  - Share and Collaborate 72

Chapter 16: Closing Off 73

- Summary of Key Concepts 73
  - Introduction to C# Programming 73
  - Understanding C# Syntax 73
  - Working with Data Types and Variables 73
  - Operators and Expressions 73
  - Control Flow and Decision Making 73
  - Arrays and Collections 73
  - Methods and Functions 73
  - Object-Oriented Programming (OOP) Basics 73
  - Exception Handling 73
  - File I/O and Serialization 73
  - Introduction to Asynchronous Programming 74
  - Working with Databases 74
  - Introduction to Web Development with C# 74

- C# 12 Features 74
- Best Practices and Tips 74
- Further Resources for Continued Learning 74
  - Books 74
  - Online Courses 74
  - Tutorials and Documentation 74
  - Open-Source Projects 74
  - Community Forums 74
- Final Thoughts 75

Chapter 1: Introduction to C#

Our comprehensive guide to learning and mastering C# programming begins with a brief overview of its purpose and scope as well as an overview of what to expect on your journey with the language.

You can access or download the code from Ziggy Rafiq GitHub Repository

https://github.com/ziggyrafiq/CSharp-12-Essentials-Guide

Purpose of the Book

In this book, readers will gain the knowledge and skills that will enable them to become proficient in programming in C#. No matter if you are a beginner just getting started with programming or an experienced developer looking to improve your skills, you'll find everything you need in this book.

Scope of the Book

From basics to more advanced topics, we will cover a broad range of topics in this book. Here's a brief outline of the key areas we'll cover:

Essential Concepts

In this lesson, we will cover the fundamentals of C# programming, including variables, data types, control flow, and methods.

Object-Oriented Programming (OOP)

Our next topic will be object-oriented programming, including classes, inheritance, polymorphism, and encapsulation.

Web Development with C#

You will learn how to create dynamic web applications using C# and ASP.NET, covering topics such as MVC architecture, web forms, and data access.

Advanced Topics

The course covers advanced topics such as asynchronous programming, working with databases, and leveraging C# 12 features to write more efficient and expressive code.

Best Practices and Tips

We'll discuss coding standards, performance optimization techniques, debugging strategies, and other best practices to help you write clean, maintainable, and efficient code throughout the book.

What to Expect

Using snippets of code, illustrations, and real-life situations to reinforce your understanding of C# programming, this book is planned to give you a blend of theoretical concepts, practical examples, and hands-on exercises.

Let's Get Started

Now that you know what to expect, it's time to dive into the exciting world of C# programming! Whether you want to create desktop applications, web services, or games, C# provides a flexible and powerful development platform.

Get ready to embark on an enriching learning experience and unlock the full potential of C# programming as we explore the foundational concepts of C# programming in the next chapters!

Brief History of the C# Programming Language

Key Milestones

Introduction in 2000
C# was introduced in 2000 along with Microsoft's .NET framework, positioning itself as an important component for the future of software development.

Designed by Anders Hejlsberg
A renowned software engineer known for his work on Turbo Pascal and Delphi, Anders Hejlsberg primarily designed this language. By combining the best aspects of existing languages with innovative concepts, he created a language with his expertise in language design.

Evolution and Growth
Throughout the years, C# has evolved into a versatile and widely-used language for building desktop applications, web applications, games, mobile apps, and more.

Impact and Significance
In shaping the modern landscape of programming languages, C# has played a pivotal role in transforming the software development industry.

Windows applications, web services, and enterprise solutions have been built with it thanks to its integration with the .NET framework.

Overview of the C# Programming Language

Key Features

Modern Language
The C# language is designed to be a modern programming language, incorporating features and concepts from C++, Java, and Delphi.

Object-Oriented
C# follows the principles of object-oriented programming (OOP), allowing developers to create classes, objects, and interfaces that model real-world entities and encapsulate data and behavior.

Strong Typing
C# is a statically typed language, which means variables must be declared with their data types at compile time.

Advantages of C#

Simplicity
C#'s simplicity and readability make it easier for developers to write, understand, and maintain code.

Scalability
C# is highly scalable and can be used to create small console applications, large enterprise systems, and everything in between.

Rich Features
A rich set of features in C#, including generics, LINQ (Language Integrated Query), asynchronous programming, and more, enable developers to write efficient and expressive code.

Importance of Mastering C# for Both Beginners and Experts

For Beginners

Gentle Learning Curve
Due to its straightforward syntax and intuitive language features, C# offers a gentle learning curve for beginners.

Extensive Documentation
It is easy for beginners to find answers, solve problems, and learn new concepts with C#'s extensive documentation and resources online.

Gateway to Software Development
Learn C# and open the door to a wide range of career opportunities in software development.

For Experts

Advanced Features and Tools
A rich set of advanced features and tools is available in C# to meet the needs of experienced developers.

Versatility
C# is a versatile language that can be used to build a wide range of applications, including web applications, desktop software, games, and mobile applications.

Career Advancement
A mastery of C# can lead to career advancement opportunities for experienced developers.

Importance and Relevance in Modern Software Development

Widely Used Across Domains

Versatility
It is widely used in a wide range of fields such as web development, game development, mobile app development, and enterprise software development.

Ubiquitous Presence
C# is ubiquitous across a wide range of industries and sectors, powering mission-critical applications and services in finance, healthcare, and education.

Integration with the .NET Framework
Robust Ecosystem
C# is deeply integrated with the .NET framework, which allows you to build and deploy applications across different platforms and devices.

Platform Independence
The advent of .NET Core and the recent transition to .NET 5 and beyond have made C# platform-independent, allowing developers to target a wide range of platforms.

New Features and Enhancements in C# 12
Continuous Improvement
With C# 12, a number of new features and enhancements have been added to further enhance the language's productivity and code quality.

Improved Productivity
New features such as pattern-matching enhancements, record types, and switch expressions streamline common programming tasks.

By exploring the world of C# programming, you'll discover how vast the opportunities for software development are.

Chapter 2: Getting Started with C#

Setting up the Development Environment

You must set up your development environment properly before diving into C# programming. In this section, we'll walk you through the process of installing and configuring the necessary tools.

Introduction

A well-configured environment is essential for efficient C# programming. In this section, we will provide an overview of how to set up your environment correctly.

Required Tools

The .NET SDK and Visual Studio are required tools to begin programming in C#. .NET SDK is a runtime and libraries for building .NET applications, while Visual Studio is an integrated development environment (IDE) that provides tools for C# development.

Step-by-Step Guide

We'll guide you through downloading, installing, and configuring Visual Studio and .NET SDK, whether you're using Windows, macOS, or Linux to ensure you're ready to start coding C#.

Basic Syntax and Structure of C# Programs

A basic understanding of the syntax and structure of C# programs is essential to writing correct and efficient code.

Introduction

You will learn about keywords, data types, variables, and operators. Understanding these elements is crucial to writing C# programs.

Control Flow Statements

In this lesson, we'll explain how control flow statements, such as if-else, switch, while, and for loops, are used to control execution flow within your program. We'll also provide examples that illustrate their use.

Writing and Running Your First C# Program

Once you've set up your development environment and learned the basics of C# programming, you're ready to write and run your first C# program.

Step-by-Step Guide

This step-by-step guide will guide you through the process of creating a new Visual Studio project and writing your first C# program. You will learn how to navigate the Visual Studio interface, create a new project, and write C# code.

"Hello World" Program

Using the C# language, we will create a simple "Hello World" program to teach you the basics of C# programming. We will also discuss console output, variable declaration, and basic syntax rules.

Understanding Basic Syntax and Structure

The purpose of this chapter is to deepen our understanding of the basic syntax and structure of C# programs, covering advanced topics such as namespaces, classes, objects, and access modifiers.

In-depth Explanation

We will provide a detailed explanation of C# namespaces, classes, and objects. You will learn how to define classes, create objects, and organize your code using namespaces.

Access Modifiers

The notions of public, private, and protected play a crucial role in controlling access to class members. We'll discuss how they work and how they relate to object-oriented programming.

Constructors, Properties, and Methods

As building blocks of classes, constructors create objects, properties store data, and methods define behavior. We will explore how these three elements work together.

This chapter has provided you with a solid foundation in C# programming, including how to set up your development environment and how to understand the basic syntax and structure. Once you have this knowledge, you can begin building your own C# applications and tackle more advanced topics.

Chapter 3: Data Types and Variables

Understanding data types and variables in C# is crucial to write efficient and reliable code. This chapter will cover the fundamentals of C# data types and variables. Our first step will be to examine primitive data types, followed by variable declarations and initialisation, and then type conversion and casting. Moreover, we will discuss the importance of choosing the right data types and variables for optimal performance.

Primitive Data Types

We'll look at some of the most commonly used primitive data types for representing data in C#. Primitive data types are predefined by the language and have fixed sizes in memory.

int: An integer represents a number.

float: Single-precision floating-point numbers are represented by this type.

double: Double-precision floating-point numbers are represented by this type.

bool: This value represents a Boolean value (true or false).

You must understand the characteristics of the different data types, such as the number of values they can hold and how much memory they occupy, so you can select the appropriate data type for your variables.

Declaring and Initializing Variables

Using variables is an excellent way to store and manipulate data in C#. Before using a variable, it must be declared, specifying its data type. C# variables are declared with the following syntax: **dataType variableName**;

Below are the code examples of this.

int age; // Declaring an integer variable named 'age'

Whenever a variable is declared, it can be initialised by assigning it a value. You can do this at the point of declaration or later in the program.

int age = 30; // Initializing 'age' with the value 30

Variables can be initialised automatically or explicitly depending on your program's context and requirements.

Type Conversion and Casting

Type conversion is the process of converting a value from one data type to another. There are two types of type conversions in C#: implicit and explicit. Explicit type conversion (also known as casting) occurs explicitly when there is no risk of data loss, but implicit type conversion occurs automatically when there is no risk of data loss.

```
 int numberInteger = 10;
Console.WriteLine($"This is the integer number result in C# {numberInteger}");

// Implicit conversion from int to double
//double numberDouble = numInt;

double number = 3.14;
// Explicit conversion from double to int (casting)
int roundedNum = (int)number;

Console.WriteLine($"This is the rounded number result used casting in C# {roundedNum}");
```

To work with different data types and to ensure the correctness of your programs, you must understand when and how to perform type conversions.

Importance of Understanding Data Types and Variables

By selecting the right data types and variables, you can minimise memory consumption and improve the performance of your programs. By choosing appropriate data types, you can maximise memory usage and program efficiency. Additionally, understanding data types helps in writing clear and maintainable code, making it easier for other developers to understand and collaborate on your projects.

Best Practices for Working with Data Types and Variables

To ensure code clarity and maintainability when working with data types and variables, it's essential to follow best practices. Code readability and understanding of variable purposes are improved by descriptive variable naming and adherence to naming conventions. Also, ensuring your code is reliable requires proper initialisation of variables and careful handling of type conversions.

The concepts covered in this chapter will help you understand C#'s data types and variables, as well as how to work with them effectively. To write efficient, reliable, and maintainable C# code, you must understand these fundamentals.

Chapter 4: Operators and Expressions

C# operators and expressions are the focus of this chapter. We will explore the various types of operators available in C#, understand their precedence and associativity rules, and understand how to use expressions effectively in C# programs. As well as discussing the importance of mastering operators and expressions, we'll share some tips for using them effectively.

Arithmetic, Relational, Logical, and Bitwise Operators

An operator in C# executes an operation on an operand. There are several types of operators in C#, including arithmetic operators, relational operators, logical operators, and bitwise operators.

Arithmetic Operators

The arithmetic operators perform mathematical calculations such as additions, subtractions, multiplications, divisions, and modulus.

```
/*********************************************************************
* Arithmetic Operators  Code Examples                               *
*********************************************************************/
int a = 10;
int b = 5;

// Addition
int sum = a + b;
Console.WriteLine($"The result for Addition is {sum}");

// Subtraction
int difference = a - b;
Console.WriteLine($"The result for Subtraction is {difference}");

// Multiplication
int product = a * b;
Console.WriteLine($"The result for Multiplication is {product}");

// Division
int quotient = a / b;
Console.WriteLine($"The result for Division is {quotient}");

// Modulus
int remainder = a % b;
Console.WriteLine($"The result for Modulus is {remainder}");
```

Relational Operators

Comparing two values and determining their relationships can be accomplished using relational operators.

```
/*********************************************************************
 * Relational Operators  Code Examples                               *
 *********************************************************************/

int x = 10;
int y = 20;

// Equal to
bool isEqual = x == y;
Console.WriteLine($"The result for  Equal to is {isEqual}");

// Not equal to
bool isNotEqual = x != y;
Console.WriteLine($"The result for  Not equal to is {isNotEqual}");

// Greater than
bool isGreater = x > y;
Console.WriteLine($"The result for Greater than is {isGreater}");

// Less than
bool isLess = x < y;
Console.WriteLine($"The result for Less than is {isLess}");

// Greater than or equal to
bool isGreaterOrEqual = x >= y;
Console.WriteLine($"The result for Greater than or equal to is {isGreaterOrEqual}");

// Less than or equal to
bool isLessOrEqual = x <= y;
Console.WriteLine($"The result for Less than or equal to is {isLessOrEqual}");
```

Logical Operators

The logical operators can be used to determine whether a boolean value is true or false.

```
/*********************************************************************
 * Logical Operators Code Examples                                   *
 *********************************************************************/
bool isTrue = true;
bool isFalse = false;

// Logical AND
bool logicalAnd = isTrue && isFalse;
Console.WriteLine($"The result forLogical AND is {logicalAnd}");

// Logical OR
bool logicalOr = isTrue || isFalse;
Console.WriteLine($"The result for Logical OR is {logicalOr}");

// Logical NOT
bool logicalNot = !isTrue;
Console.WriteLine($"The result for Logical NOT is {logicalNot}");
```

Bitwise Operators

In bitwise operations, operations are performed at the level of bits.

```
/***********************************************************
 * Bitwise Operators Code Examples                         *
 ***********************************************************/
// Binary representation: 0101
int p = 5;

// Binary representation: 0011
int q = 3;

// Bitwise AND (result: 1)
int bitwiseAnd = p & q;
Console.WriteLine($"The result for Bitwise AND is {bitwiseAnd}");


// Bitwise OR (result: 7)
int bitwiseOr = p | q;
Console.WriteLine($"The result for Bitwise OR  is {bitwiseOr}");

// Bitwise XOR (result: 6)
int bitwiseXor = p ^ q;
Console.WriteLine($"The result for Bitwise XOR is {bitwiseXor}");

// Bitwise complement (result: -6)
int bitwiseComplement = ~p;
Console.WriteLine($"The result for Bitwise complement is {bitwiseComplement}");


// Left shift (result: 10)
int leftShift = p << 1;
Console.WriteLine($"The result for  Left shift is {leftShift}");

// Right shift (result: 2)
int rightShift = p >> 1;
Console.WriteLine($"The result for  Right shift is {rightShift}");
```

Precedence and Associativity Rules

Operators have precedence levels in C# that determine their order of evaluation within an expression. Additionally, operators with the same precedence level can have a right-to-left associativity or a left-to-right associativity.

Similarly, in a multiplication equation 2+3*4, the multiplication operation comes first, resulting in 2+3.

```
// Result: 14
int result = 2 + 3 * 4;
Console.WriteLine($"The result is {result}");
```

The order of evaluation can be explicitly specified using parentheses to override the default precedence.

```
// Result: 20
int result = (2 + 3) * 4;
Console.WriteLine($"The result is {result}");
```

Using Expressions in C# Programs
A C# program is built around expressions, which combine operators and operands to compute and return values.

```
/**********************************************************************
*Using Expressions in C# Programs                                     *
**********************************************************************/
int x = 10;
int y = 5;

// Expression
int result = (x + y) * (x - y);

// Output: 75
Console.WriteLine($"The result is {result}");
```

C# programs can use expressions to perform various tasks, including assignments, method calls, conditional statements, and loops.

Importance of Understanding Operators and Expressions
Programmers depend on operators and expressions to carry out computations, make decisions, and manipulate data efficiently and effectively. Understanding how operators and expressions work is crucial to writing code that is readable and efficient.

Best Practices for Working with Operators and Expressions
In complex expressions, parentheses are useful for clarifying the order of evaluation and ensuring the intended outcome. Additionally, logically organizing expressions can enhance code clarity.

```
/**********************************************************************
*Best Practices for Working with Operators and Expressions            *
**********************************************************************/
int c = 3;
int d = 15;
int e = 50;
int x = 10;
int y = 5;

int result = (a + b) * c - (d / e);
Console.WriteLine($"The result is {result}");
```

With these best practices, developers can write code that is easier to comprehend, debug, and maintain, resulting in more robust and reliable software.

Chapter 5: Control Flow and Decision-Making

In this chapter, we'll examine control flow and decision-making structures in C#. We'll learn about conditional statements such as if, else, and switch, as well as looping structures such as for, while, and do-while. In addition, we'll share tips and tricks on how to work effectively with control flow and decision-making.

Conditional Statements (if, else, switch)

We can use conditional statements to make decisions based on certain conditions. In C#, we have three types of conditional statements: if, else, and switch.

if Statement

In an if statement, a condition is evaluated and a block of code is executed if the condition is true.

```
/**********************************************************************
* if Statement  Code Examples                                         *
**********************************************************************/
int num = 10;
if (num > 0)
{
    Console.WriteLine("Number is positive");
}
```

else Statement

When the condition is false, the else statement is used to execute a different block of code.

```
/**********************************************************************
* else Statement  Code Example                                        *
**********************************************************************/
int num = -5;
if (num > 0)
{
    Console.WriteLine("Number is positive");
}
else
{
    Console.WriteLine("Number is negative");
}
```

switch Statement

With the switch statement, we can select which code block should be executed based on the value of a variable.

```
/********************************************************************
* switch Statement  Code Example                                    *
********************************************************************/
int day = 3;
switch (day)
{
   case 1:
      Console.WriteLine("Sunday");
      break;
   case 2:
      Console.WriteLine("Monday");
      break;
   // More cases...
   default:
      Console.WriteLine("Invalid day");
      break;
}
```

Looping Structures (for, while, do-while)

A looping structure is used to repeat a block of code multiple times. C# provides three looping structures: for, while, and do-while.

for Loop

In a for loop, a block of code is repeated a certain number of times.

```
/********************************************************************
* for Loop  Code Example                                            *
********************************************************************/
for (int i = 0; i < 5; i++)
{
   Console.WriteLine(i);
}
```

while Loop

In a while loop, a block of code is repeated until a specific condition is met.

```
/********************************************************************
* while Loop  Code Example                                          *
********************************************************************/
int i = 0;
while (i < 5)
{
   Console.WriteLine(i);
   i++;
}
```

do-while Loop

Unlike the while loop, the do-while loop always executes the block of code at least once before checking the condition.

```
/***********************************************************************
 * do-while Loop  Code Example                                         *
 ***********************************************************************/
int i = 0;
do
{
    Console.WriteLine(i);
    i++;
} while (i < 5);
```

Branching and Control Flow Mechanisms

We can implement various algorithms and solve complex programming problems by using control flow mechanisms, such as conditional statements and loops.

```
//Branching and Control Flow Mechanisms
int num = 10;
if (num > 0)
{
    Console.WriteLine("Number is positive");
}
else
{
    Console.WriteLine("Number is negative");
}

for (int i = 0; i < 5; i++)
{
    Console.WriteLine(i);
}
```

Importance of Understanding Control Flow and Decision-Making

To design algorithms, implement logic, and write efficient and structured code, one must understand control flow and decision-making structures. By mastering these concepts, developers can develop programs that can handle a variety of scenarios and adapt to a variety of situations.

Best Practices for Working with Control Flow and Decision-Making

The structure of control flow structures must be chosen based on the problem's requirements when working with them. It is also easier for other developers to understand and modify code when control flow structures are organized in a clear, structured manner, increasing readability and maintainability.

```
if (condition)

{

   // Code block

}

else if (anotherCondition)

{

   // Code block

}

else

{

   // Code block

}
```

Developers can write code that is not only functional, but also easy to understand, maintain, and debug by following these best practices.

We will discuss advanced topics in C# programming in the following chapters, building upon the basics of control flow and decision-making covered in this chapter.

Chapter 6: Arrays and Collections

In this chapter, we'll explore the concepts of arrays and collections in C#. We'll learn about single-dimensional and multi-dimensional arrays, as well as various collection types, including lists, dictionaries, queues, and stacks. We'll also discuss how to manipulate, iterate, and sort collections.

Arrays: Single-Dimensional, Multi-Dimensional

C# arrays can store multiple values of the same type in a contiguous memory block. They can be single-dimensional or multidimensional.

Single-Dimensional Arrays

The elements of a single-dimensional array are stored in a linear order.

```
/**********************************************************************
* Single-Dimensional Arrays Code Examples                             *
**********************************************************************/

// Declaration and initialization
int[] numbers = new int[5];
numbers[0] = 10;
numbers[1] = 20;

// Accessing elements and Output: 10
Console.WriteLine(numbers[0]);
```

Multi-Dimensional Arrays

An array with multiple dimensions, such as rows and columns, is called a multi-dimensional array.

```
/**********************************************************************
* Multi-Dimensional Arrays Code Example                               *
**********************************************************************/

// Declaration and initialization
int[,] matrix = new int[2, 3];
matrix[0, 0] = 1;
matrix[0, 1] = 2;

// Accessing elements Output 1
Console.WriteLine(matrix[0, 0]);
```

Lists, Dictionaries, and Other Collection Types

A collection in C# provides a flexible way to store and manipulate collections of data. Common collections include lists, dictionaries, queues, and stacks.

Lists

Lists: Lists allow dynamic resizing and provide methods for adding, removing, and accessing elements.

```
/********************************************************************
 * List Code Example                                                 *
 ********************************************************************/
// Declaration and initialization
List<int> numbersList = new List<int>();
numbersList.Add(10);
numbersList.Add(20);
// Accessing elements Output: 10
Console.WriteLine(numbers[0]);
```

Dictionaries

The purpose of dictionaries is to store key-value pairs and provide fast lookup based on keys.

```
/********************************************************************
 * Dictionaries Code Examples                                        *
 ********************************************************************/
// Declaration and initialization
Dictionary<string, int> ages = new Dictionary<string, int>();
ages["Alice"] = 30;
ages["Bob"] = 25;

// Accessing elements Output: 30
Console.WriteLine(ages["Alice"]);
```

Working with Collections: Iteration, Manipulation, Sorting

In addition to iterating over elements, collections support manipulation (adding, removing, and modifying).

```
/********************************************************************
 * Iteration, Manipulation, Sorting Code Examples                    *
 ********************************************************************/
List<int> numbersListLoop = new List<int>() { 3, 1, 2 };

// Iterating over elements
foreach (int num in numbersListLoop)
{
    Console.WriteLine(num);
}
// Sorting
numbersListLoop.Sort();
```

Declaring and Initializing Arrays

The C# language supports a number of syntaxes for declaring and initializing arrays.

```
/*********************************************************************
* Declaring and Initializing Arrays Code Examples                    *
*********************************************************************/
// Declaration and initialization
int[] numbers1 = new int[3];

// Initialization with explicit values
int[] numbers2 = new int[] { 1, 2, 3 };

// Implicit initialization
int[] numbers3 = { 1, 2, 3 };
```

Working with Multidimensional Arrays

When you want to represent data in more than one dimension, you can use multidimensional arrays.

```
/*********************************************************************
* Working with Multidimensional Arrays Code Examples                 *
*********************************************************************/

// Declaration and initialization
int[,] matrixMultidimensional = new int[2, 3];
matrixMultidimensional[0, 0] = 1;
matrixMultidimensional[0, 1] = 2;

// Accessing elements Output: 1
Console.WriteLine(matrixMultidimensional[0, 0]);
```

Introduction to Collections

With C# collections, you can manage data in a powerful way, offering a variety of types to fit your needs.

```
/********************************************************************
* Introduction to Collections Code Example                          *
********************************************************************/
// Initialize the collections
List<string> names = new List<string>();
Dictionary<string, int> agesCollection = new Dictionary<string, int>();
Queue<int> queue = new Queue<int>();
Stack<int> stack = new Stack<int>();

// Add elements to the List
names.Add("Alice");
names.Add("Bob");
names.Add("Charlie");

// Display elements in the List
Console.WriteLine("Names in the List:");
foreach (string name in names)
{
    Console.WriteLine(name);
}

// Add elements to the Dictionary
agesCollection["Alice"] = 30;
agesCollection["Bob"] = 25;
agesCollection["Charlie"] = 35;

// Display elements in the Dictionary
Console.WriteLine("\nAges in the Dictionary:");
foreach (KeyValuePair<string, int> entry in agesCollection)
{
    Console.WriteLine($"{entry.Key}: {entry.Value}");
}

// Add elements to the Queue
queue.Enqueue(10);
queue.Enqueue(20);
queue.Enqueue(30);

// Display elements in the Queue
Console.WriteLine("\nElements in the Queue:");
while (queue.Count > 0)
{
    Console.WriteLine(queue.Dequeue());
}
```

```csharp
// Add elements to the Stack
stack.Push(100);
stack.Push(200);
stack.Push(300);

// Display elements in the Stack
Console.WriteLine("\nElements in the Stack:");
while (stack.Count > 0)
{
    Console.WriteLine(stack.Pop());
}
```

Arrays and collections in C# have been covered in this chapter in depth. You will be able to handle complex data structures and solve a wide range of programming problems if you master these concepts and master their use.

Chapter 7: Methods and Functions

The purpose of this chapter is to introduce the concept of methods and functions in C#. In addition, we will discuss the importance of methods in programming, and how to declare and call methods, pass parameters, and return values.

Declaring and Calling Methods

Functions, also known as methods, are sets of instructions that perform specific tasks. They are defined within classes and can be called to execute their functionality.

```csharp
/*********************************************************************
* Declaring and Calling Methods Example                              *
*********************************************************************/
namespace MethodMastery;

 public class Calculator
    {   // Method declaration
        public int Add(int a, int b)
        {
           return a + b;
        }

    }
using MethodMastery;

Console.WriteLine("Hello, from Ziggy Rafiq");
Console.WriteLine("This Code Example Project is for Chapter 7");


/*********************************************************************
* Declaring and Calling Methods Example                              *
*********************************************************************/
// Calling the method
Calculator calc = new Calculator();

// Output: 8
int sum = calc.Add(5, 3);

Console.WriteLine($"The result of this is {sum}");
```

Passing Parameters: Value vs. Reference

Whether a parameter is passed by value or by reference depends on which type of parameter it is. When passed by value, a copy of the parameter's value is passed to the method.

```csharp
/**********************************************************************
* Declaring and Calling Methods Example                               *
**********************************************************************/
namespace MethodMastery;

public class Calculator
  {
     public void ModifyValue(int x)
     {
        x = 10;
     }

     public void ModifyReference(ref int x)
     {
        x = 10;
     }



  }

using MethodMastery;

Console.WriteLine("Hello, from Ziggy Rafiq");
Console.WriteLine("This Code Example Project is for Chapter 7");

/**********************************************************************
* Declaring and Calling Methods Example                               *
**********************************************************************/
// Calling the method
Calculator calc = new Calculator();

int number = 5;
calc.ModifyValue(number);

// Output: 5 (unchanged)
Console.WriteLine($"The result of this is {number}");

calc.ModifyReference(ref number);

// Output: 10 (modified)
Console.WriteLine($"The result of this is {number}");
```

Returning Values from Methods

Return statements allow methods to return values. A return type indicates the type of value returned by a method.

```
/********************************************************************
* Declaring and Calling Methods Example                             *
********************************************************************/
namespace MethodMastery;
  public class Calculator
  {
     public int Multiply(int a, int b)
     {
        return a * b;
     }

  }



using MethodMastery;

Console.WriteLine("Hello, from Ziggy Rafiq");
Console.WriteLine("This Code Example Project is for Chapter 7");

/********************************************************************
* Declaring and Calling Methods Example                             *
********************************************************************/
// Calling the method
Calculator calc = new Calculator();

// Output: 12
int result = calc.Multiply(4, 3);
Console.WriteLine($"The result of this is {result}");
```

Handling Method Overloading

With method overloading, we can define multiple methods with the same name but different parameter lists, so that we can provide different functionality depending on the parameters.

```
namespace MethodMastery;

public class Printer
{
   public void Print(string message)
   {
      Console.WriteLine(message);
   }

   public void Print(int number)
   {
      Console.WriteLine(number);
   }

}
```

```
using MethodMastery;

Console.WriteLine("Hello, from Ziggy Rafiq");
Console.WriteLine("This Code Example Project is for Chapter 7");

/***********************************************************************
 * Handling Method Overloading Code Example                            *
 ***********************************************************************/

Printer printer = new Printer();
// Output: Hello
printer.Print("Hello");

// Output: 5
printer.Print(5);
```

Importance of Methods and Functions

Methods help us organize code, reusability, and readability. They encapsulate functionality and make our code easier to understand and maintain by encapsulating functionality.

Best Practices for Working with Methods and Functions

Keeping code clear and maintainable requires following best practices. This includes naming methods descriptively, defining clear method signatures, and adhering to naming conventions.

Developing a deep understanding of methods and functions will help you write code that is more modular, maintainable, and scalable, which helps you accomplish complex tasks with confidence.

Chapter 8: Object-Oriented Programming (OOP) Basics

In this chapter, we'll dive into the fundamentals of Object-Oriented Programming (OOP) in C#. The topic will include classes, objects, encapsulation, inheritance, polymorphism, constructors, destructors, and access modifiers, as well as the importance of OOP principles.

Classes and Objects

A class is the basic building block of Object Oriented Programming in C#, serving as a blueprint for creating objects, defining their structure, and specifying their behavior.

```
/********************************************************************
 * Classes and Objects Code Example                                  *
 ********************************************************************/
namespace OOPExplorer;

public class Car
{
    // Class members
    public string Make;
    public string Model;
    public int Year;


    // Constructor
    public Car(string make, string model, int year)
    {
        Make = make;
        Model = model;
        Year = year;
    }

}
using OOPExplorer;

Console.WriteLine("Hello, from Ziggy Rafiq");
Console.WriteLine("This Code Example Project is for Chapter 8");


/********************************************************************
 * Classes and Objects Code Example                                  *
 ********************************************************************/
// Creating objects
Car myCar = new Car("Toyota", "Camry", 2022);
Console.WriteLine($"My car is {myCar.Make}, Model is{myCar.Model} and the year is {myCar.Year}");
```

Encapsulation, Inheritance, Polymorphism

The principles of OOP include encapsulation, inheritance, and polymorphism.

```
/*********************************************************************
 * Encapsulation Code Example                                        *
 *********************************************************************/

namespace OOPExplorer;
public class Person
{
   private string name;

   public string Name
   {
      get { return name; }
      set { name = value; }
   }
}




/*********************************************************************
 * Inheritance Code Example                                          *
 *********************************************************************/
namespace OOPExplorer;

public class Student : Person
{
   public Guid StudentID { get; set; }
}
```

```csharp
using OOPExplorer;

/*********************************************************************
 * Encapsulation and Inheritance Code Example                        *
 *********************************************************************/
// Creating object
Student student = new Student();
Console.WriteLine($"The Student ID is {student.StudentID}/n");
Console.WriteLine($"The Student name is {student.Name}/n");

/*********************************************************************
 * Polymorphism Code Example                                         *
 *********************************************************************/
namespace OOPExplorer;

public class Animal
{
    public virtual void MakeSound()
    {
        Console.WriteLine("Some generic sound");
    }
}



/*********************************************************************
 * Polymorphism Code Example                                         *
 *********************************************************************/
namespace OOPExplorer;

public class Dog:Animal
{
    public override void MakeSound()
    {
        Console.WriteLine("Woof!");
    }

}



using OOPExplorer;

Console.WriteLine("Hello, from Ziggy Rafiq");
Console.WriteLine("This Code Example Project is for Chapter 8");

/*********************************************************************
 * Polymorphism Code Example                                         *
 *********************************************************************/

Animal animal = new Animal();
Console.WriteLine($"Animal sound is {animal.MakeSound}/n");

Dog dog = new Dog();
Console.WriteLine($"Dog sound is {dog.MakeSound}/n");
```

Constructors and Destructors

As an example of a constructor, a constructor is a method that initializes an object when it is created. As an example of a destructor, a destructor is a method that cleans up resources when objects are destroyed.

```
/***********************************************************************
 * Encapsulation Code Example                                          *
 ***********************************************************************/

namespace OOPExplorer;
public class Person
{
    public Person()
    {
        Console.WriteLine("Constructor called");
    }

    ~Person()
    {
        Console.WriteLine("Destructor called");
    }

}

using OOPExplorer;

Console.WriteLine("Hello, from Ziggy Rafiq");
Console.WriteLine("This Code Example Project is for Chapter 8");


/***********************************************************************
 * Constructors and Destructors Code Example                           *
 ***********************************************************************/
Person person = new Person();
// Explicitly trigger garbage collection for demonstration purposes
// Dereference the object to make it eligible for garbage collection
person = null;

// Force garbage collection
GC.Collect();

// Wait for the destructor to be called
GC.WaitForPendingFinalizers();
```

Access Modifiers and Visibility

It is possible to control the visibility and accessibility of class members using access modifiers.

```
public class Example
{
    public int PublicMember;

    private int PrivateMember;

    protected int ProtectedMember;

    internal int InternalMember;

    protected internal int ProtectedInternalMember;
}
```

Importance of OOP Principles

By designing classes with clear responsibilities and well-defined interfaces, we can create flexible, extensible, and maintainable code.

Best Practices for Implementing OOP Concepts

Implementing OOP concepts requires designing classes with clear responsibilities and well-defined interfaces. By utilizing encapsulation, inheritance, and polymorphism effectively, we can create flexible and extensible code that adapts to changing requirements and promotes reuse.

Chapter 9: Exception Handling

To write robust and reliable software in C#, exception handling is crucial. We will explore different ways to handle exceptions in this chapter, including try-catch blocks, throwing and catching exceptions, handling specific types of exceptions, using try-catch-finally blocks, defining custom exception classes, and best practices.

Handling Exceptions Using try-catch Blocks

By using try-catch blocks, exceptions can be gracefully handled during program execution.

```csharp
try
{
    // Code that may throw an exception
    int result = 10 / 0;
}
catch (Exception ex)
{
    // Handle the exception
    Console.WriteLine($"An error occurred: {ex.Message}");
}
```

Throwing and Catching Exceptions

Throwing exceptions indicates errors or exceptional conditions, and catching them gracefully handles them.

```csharp
try
{
    throw new Exception("Something went wrong");
}
catch (Exception ex)
{
    Console.WriteLine($"An error occurred: {ex.Message}");
}
```

Handling and Throwing Exceptions in C#

C# exceptions can occur in a number of scenarios, such as null reference exceptions, index out of range exceptions, or file IO exceptions.

```csharp
try
{
    int[] numbers = null;
    int sum = numbers.Sum(); // Throws NullReferenceException
}
catch (NullReferenceException ex)
{
    Console.WriteLine($"Null reference exception: {ex.Message}");
}
```

try-catch-finally Blocks

Regardless of whether an exception occurs, cleanup operations can be performed in the try-catch-finally block.

```csharp
try
{
    // Code that may throw an exception
}
catch (Exception ex)
{
    // Handle the exception
}
finally
{
    // Cleanup operations
}
```

Custom Exception Classes

To represent application-specific error conditions, custom exception classes can be defined.

```csharp
namespace ExceptionExplorer;

public class CustomException : Exception
{
    public CustomException(string message) : base(message)
    {
    }
}
```

```csharp
/**********************************************************************
 * Custom Exception Code Example                                      *
 **********************************************************************/
try
{
    // Throw the custom exception
    throw new ExceptionExplorer.CustomException("This is a custom exception.");
}
catch (ExceptionExplorer.CustomException ex)
{
    // Catch and handle the custom exception
    Console.WriteLine(ex.Message);
}
```

Best Practices for Exception Handling

In order to ensure robust error handling, it is essential to follow best practices when designing exception handling mechanisms.

```
/**********************************************************
* Best Practices for Exception Handling Code Example      *
**********************************************************/
// Configure Serilog to write log messages to the console
Log.Logger = new LoggerConfiguration()
   .WriteTo.Console()
   .CreateLogger();
try
{
   // Code that may throw an exception
}
catch (Exception ex)
{
   // Log the exception
   // Provide user-friendly error message
   Log.Error(ex, "An error occurred/n");
   Log.Error($"{ex.Message} /n");
   Log.Error($"{ex.StackTrace} /n");
   Console.WriteLine("An error occurred. Please contact support.");


   // Throw the exception (optional)
   throw;
}
```

When you master exception handling techniques and follow best practices, you can build software that gracefully handles errors and exceptions encountered during runtime.

Chapter 10: File I/O and Serialization

Many software applications require input/output (I/O) and object serialization. In this chapter, we'll explore how to perform file I/O tasks, work with streams and readers/writers, serialize and deserialize objects, handle exceptions in file operations, and follow best practices for efficient and reliable file I/O and serialization.

Reading from and Writing to Files

The process of reading data from files and writing data to files is common in many applications.

```csharp
Console.WriteLine("Hello, from Ziggy Rafiq");
Console.WriteLine("This Code Example Project is for Chapter 10");

/**********************************************************************
 * Writing data to a text file Code Example                           *
 **********************************************************************/

using (StreamWriter writer = new StreamWriter("dummy-file.txt"))
{
    writer.WriteLine("Hello, from Ziggy Rafiq!");
}

/**********************************************************************
 * Reading data from a text file Code Example                         *
 **********************************************************************/
using (StreamReader reader = new StreamReader("data.txt"))
{
    string line = reader.ReadLine();
    Console.WriteLine(line); // Output: Hello, World!
}
```

Working with Streams and Readers/Writers

The use of streams can be used to perform general input/output operations, while the use of readers/writers enables working with text at a higher level of abstraction.

```csharp
/***********************************************************************
* Writing data to a binary file using FileStream Code Example          *
***********************************************************************/
using (FileStream stream = new FileStream("dummy-file.bin", FileMode.Create))
{
    // Hello
    byte[] data = { 0x48, 0x65, 0x6C, 0x6C, 0x6F };
    stream.Write(data, 0, data.Length);
}

/***********************************************************************
* Reading data from a binary file using FileStream  Code Example       *
***********************************************************************/
using (FileStream stream = new FileStream("dummy-file.bin", FileMode.Open))
{
    byte[] buffer = new byte[5];
    stream.Read(buffer, 0, buffer.Length);
    string text = Encoding.ASCII.GetString(buffer);
    // Output: Hello
    Console.WriteLine(text);
}
```

Serialization and Deserialization of Objects

The serialization of objects converts them into bytes for storage or transmission, and the deserialization of objects reconstructs them from the serialized data.

```csharp
/***********************************************************************
* Serialization and Deserialization of Objects  Code Example           *
***********************************************************************/
namespace FileForge;

[Serializable]
public class Person
{
    public string Name { get; set; }=string.Empty;
    public int Age { get; set; } = 0;

}
```

```csharp
/**********************************************************************
 * Serialization  Code Example                                        *
 * ********************************************************************/
// Create a Person object
Person person = new Person { Name = "Alice", Age = 30 };

try
{
    // Serialize the Person object to JSON and write it to the file
    File.WriteAllText("dummy-file.json", JsonSerializer.Serialize(person));

    Console.WriteLine("Serialization successful.");
}
catch (Exception ex)
{
    Console.WriteLine("Error occurred during serialization: " + ex.Message);
}

/**********************************************************************
 * Deserialization  Code Example                                      *
 * ********************************************************************/
try
{
    // Read the JSON string from the file and deserialize it to a Person object
    Person deserializedPerson = JsonSerializer.Deserialize<Person>(File.ReadAllText("dummy-file.json"));

    // Output the deserialized Person object
    Console.WriteLine($"Name: {deserializedPerson.Name}, Age: {deserializedPerson.Age}");
}
catch (Exception ex)
{
    Console.WriteLine("Error occurred during deserialization: " + ex.Message);
}
```

Handling Exceptions in File I/O Operations

An exception can be thrown during file I/O operations, such as a FileNotFoundException, an IOException, or an UnauthorizedAccessException.

```
/***********************************************************************
 * Handling Exceptions in File I/O Operations  Code Example             *
 * *********************************************************************/

try
{
   using (StreamWriter writer = new StreamWriter("nonexistent.txt"))
   {
      writer.WriteLine("Hello");
   }
}
catch (FileNotFoundException ex)
{
   Console.WriteLine($"File not found: {ex.Message}");
}
catch (IOException ex)
{
   Console.WriteLine($"An I/O error occurred: {ex.Message}");
}
catch (UnauthorizedAccessException ex)
{
   Console.WriteLine($"Unauthorized access: {ex.Message}");
}
```

Best Practices for File I/O and Serialization

Make sure your file I/O and serialization are as efficient and reliable as possible by following the best practices listed below:

- Automatically dispose of resources using statements.
- Exceptions should be handled gracefully, and users should receive meaningful error messages.
- Retrying or logging errors are some methods for handling errors.
- Utilize efficient serialization formats and minimize disk I/O operations to optimize performance.

It is possible to build robust and efficient applications that handle data effectively and reliably by mastering file I/O and serialization techniques and following best practices.

Chapter 11: Introduction to Asynchronous Programming

Developing responsive and scalable applications requires asynchronous programming. In this chapter, we'll explore the fundamentals of asynchronous programming in C#, including understanding asynchronous and synchronous operations, using the async and await keywords, handling asynchronous exceptions, and best practices for writing efficient asynchronous code.

Understanding Asynchronous and Synchronous Operations

It blocks the execution thread until each task has been completed in synchronous operations. As a result, asynchronous operations allow tasks to be executed concurrently, allowing the execution thread to work on other tasks while asynchronous operations complete.

```csharp
/************************************************************************
* Understanding Asynchronous and Synchronous Operations Code Example    *
* **********************************************************************/
namespace AsyncAdept;
public class OperationProcessor
{
    // Synchronous operation
    public void PerformTaskSynchronously()
    {
        // Blocks the execution thread
        Task.Delay(1000).Wait();
        Console.WriteLine("Synchronous task completed.");
    }

    // Asynchronous operation
    public async Task PerformTaskAsynchronously()
    {
        // Frees the execution thread
        await Task.Delay(1000);
        Console.WriteLine("Asynchronous task completed.");
    }
}
```

```csharp
using AsyncAdept;

/***********************************************************************
* Understanding Asynchronous and Synchronous Operations Code Example   *
* *********************************************************************/

// Create an instance of OperationProcessor
OperationProcessor processor = new OperationProcessor();

// Call the synchronous method
processor.PerformTaskSynchronously();

// Call the asynchronous method
await processor.PerformTaskAsynchronously();

Console.WriteLine("Operations completed.");
```

Using async and await Keywords

Asynchronous operations can be defined and executed in a straightforward and readable manner with the async and await keywords.

```csharp
/***********************************************************************
* Understanding Asynchronous and Synchronous Operations Code Example   *
* *********************************************************************/
namespace AsyncAdept;
public class OperationProcessor
{
    public async Task<string> DownloadDataAsync(string url)
    {
        using (HttpClient client = new HttpClient())
        {
            string data = await client.GetStringAsync(url);
            return data;
        }
    }
}
```

```csharp
using AsyncAdept;

Console.WriteLine("Hello, from Ziggy Rafiq");
Console.WriteLine("This Code Example Project is for Chapter 11");

/************************************************************************
* Understanding Asynchronous and Synchronous Operations Code Example    *
* **********************************************************************/

// Provide the URL you want to download data from
string url = "https://ziggyrafiq.com";

try
{
    // Call the asynchronous method
    string data = await processor.DownloadDataAsync(url);

    // Output the downloaded data
    Console.WriteLine("Downloaded data:");
    Console.WriteLine(data);
}
catch (Exception ex)
{
    // Handle any exceptions that may occur during the download
    Console.WriteLine($"An error occurred: {ex.Message}");
}
```

Handling Asynchronous Exceptions

Exception handling in asynchronous programming requires special consideration due to the asynchronous nature of tasks and the possibility of multiple exceptions occurring at the same time.

```csharp
/************************************************************************
* Understanding Asynchronous and Synchronous Operations Code Example    *
* **********************************************************************/
namespace AsyncAdept;
public class OperationProcessor
{
    public async Task PerformAsyncOperation()
    {
        // Simulate an asynchronous operation that may throw an exception
        await Task.Delay(1000); // Simulate some work
        throw new InvalidOperationException("Something went wrong during the asynchronous operation.");
    }

}
```

```csharp
// Provide the URL you want to download data from
string url = "https://ziggyrafiq.com";

try
{
    // Call the asynchronous method
    string data = await processor.DownloadDataAsync(url);

    // Output the downloaded data
    Console.WriteLine("Downloaded data:");
    Console.WriteLine(data);
}
catch (Exception ex)
{
    // Handle any exceptions that may occur during the download
    Console.WriteLine($"An error occurred: {ex.Message}");
}

try
{
    await processor.PerformAsyncOperation();
}
catch (Exception ex)
{
    Console.WriteLine($"An error occurred: {ex.Message}");
}
```

Asynchronous Programming with async/await

Asynchronous programming patterns, such as asynchronous methods, delegates, and lambdas, allow developers to write code that is responsive and scalable.

```csharp
/************************************************************************
* Understanding Asynchronous and Synchronous Operations Code Example    *
* **********************************************************************/
namespace AsyncAdept;
public class OperationProcessor
{
    private HttpClient _httpClient;

    public OperationProcessor()
    {
        _httpClient = new HttpClient();
    }
    public async Task<string> FetchDataAsync(string url)
    {
        try
        {
            // Perform the HTTP request asynchronously
            HttpResponseMessage response = await _httpClient.GetAsync(url);

            // Ensure the request was successful
            response.EnsureSuccessStatusCode();

            // Read the content of the response asynchronously
            return await response.Content.ReadAsStringAsync();
        }
        catch (Exception ex)
        {
            // Handle any exceptions that occurred during the operation
            Console.WriteLine($"An error occurred: {ex.Message}");
            return null;
        }
    }
}
```

```csharp
using AsyncAdept;

Console.WriteLine("Hello, from Ziggy Rafiq");
Console.WriteLine("This Code Example Project is for Chapter 11");

/************************************************************************
 * Understanding Asynchronous and Synchronous Operations Code Example   *
 * **********************************************************************/
// Provide the URL you want to download data from
string url = "https://ziggyrafiq.com";


try
{
    // Call the asynchronous method to fetch data
    string data = await processor.FetchDataAsync(url);

    // Output the fetched data
    Console.WriteLine("Fetched data:");
    Console.WriteLine(data);
}
catch (Exception ex)
{
    // Handle any exceptions that may occur during the operation
    Console.WriteLine($"An error occurred: {ex.Message}");
}
```

Best Practices for Asynchronous Programming

Make sure your asynchronous programming is efficient and reliable by following these best practices:

- When using asynchronous methods, make sure that they are used sparingly and only for operations that will truly benefit from concurrency.
- In asynchronous programming, synchronous calls should not be used to block asynchronous tasks.
- You can handle exceptions gracefully by using try-catch blocks or the Task.Exception property.
- Code readability and maintainability can be improved by using asynchronous programming patterns, such as async methods and await able delegates.

Using asynchronous programming techniques and following best practices, you will be able to build highly responsive and scalable applications in C#.

Chapter 12: Working with Databases

The purpose of this chapter is to show you how to use ADO.NET (ActiveX Data Objects .NET) to interact with databases in C#. We'll cover connecting to databases, executing SQL queries and commands, working with datasets and data readers, handling exceptions in database operations, and best practices for working with databases.

Connecting to Databases using ADO.NET

It is possible to access and manipulate data stored in databases using ADO.NET Connection objects. Let me explain how to establish connections to databases using ADO.NET Connection objects.

```csharp
using Microsoft.Data.SqlClient;
using System.Data;

namespace DataWorks;

public class DatabaseManager
{
    private const string ConnectionString = "Data Source=myServerAddress;Initial Catalog=myDatabase;User ID=myUsername;Password=myPassword;";

    public void ConnectToDatabase()
    {
        using (SqlConnection connection = new SqlConnection(ConnectionString))
        {
            connection.Open();
            Console.WriteLine("Connected to the database.");
        }
    }
}
```

Executing SQL Queries and Commands

The ADO.NET Command object enables us to execute SQL queries and commands against a database. This article shows how to execute SQL queries and commands with ADO.NET Command objects.

```csharp
using Microsoft.Data.SqlClient;
using System.Data;

namespace DataWorks;

public class DatabaseManager
{
    private const string ConnectionString = "Data Source=myServerAddress;Initial Catalog=myDatabase;User ID=myUsername;Password=myPassword;";

    public void ExecuteSqlCommand(string query)
    {
        using (SqlConnection connection = new SqlConnection(ConnectionString))
        {
            connection.Open();
            using (SqlCommand command = new SqlCommand(query, connection))
            {
                command.ExecuteNonQuery();
                Console.WriteLine("SQL command executed successfully.");
            }
        }
    }
}
```

Working with Datasets and Data Readers

Here we will see how to use DataReader and DataSet objects provided by ADO.NET for retrieving and manipulating data from databases.

```csharp
using Microsoft.Data.SqlClient;
using System.Data;

namespace DataWorks;

public class DatabaseManager
{
    private const string ConnectionString = "Data Source=myServerAddress;Initial Catalog=myDatabase;User ID=myUsername;Password=myPassword;";

    public void ReadDataUsingDataReader(string query)
    {
        using (SqlConnection connection = new SqlConnection(ConnectionString))
        {
            connection.Open();
            using (SqlCommand command = new SqlCommand(query, connection))
            {
                using (SqlDataReader reader = command.ExecuteReader())
                {
                    while (reader.Read())
                    {
                        Console.WriteLine(reader.GetString(0));
                    }
                }
            }
        }
    }
    public void ReadDataUsingDataSet(string query)
    {
        using (SqlConnection connection = new SqlConnection(ConnectionString))
        {
            connection.Open();
            using (SqlDataAdapter adapter = new SqlDataAdapter(query, connection))
            {
                DataSet dataSet = new DataSet();
                adapter.Fill(dataSet, "TableName");
                foreach (DataRow row in dataSet.Tables["TableName"].Rows)
                {
                    Console.WriteLine(row["ColumnName"]);
                }
            }
        }
    }
}
```

Handling Exceptions in Database Operations

To ensure the reliability of our applications, we need to handle database-related exceptions gracefully using try-catch blocks.

```csharp
try
{
    // Database operation code here
}
catch (SqlException ex)
{
    Console.WriteLine($"Database error: {ex.Message}");
}
catch (Exception ex)
{
    Console.WriteLine($"An error occurred: {ex.Message}");
}
```

Best Practices for Working with Databases

We should follow these best practices when creating C# applications that interact with databases:

- SQL injection attacks can be prevented by using parameterized queries.
- Once resources have been released, close all connections.
- In database operations, use transactions to ensure atomicity and consistency.
- Ensure that invalid data is not inserted into the database by validating user input.
- To track database-related issues and respond appropriately, implement logging and error handling.

The best practices listed here, as well as ADO.NET, will allow you to build robust and reliable database-driven applications in C#.

Chapter 13: Advanced Topics

Abstract Classes and Interfaces
We will explore abstract classes and interfaces in C# to learn how they are used to define contracts and common behaviour between classes.

Abstract Classes
The abstract class is a class that cannot be instantiated directly and contains abstract methods, which are methods without a body. Abstract classes serve as blueprints for derived classes to follow.

```
/**********************************************************************
 * Abstract Classes Blocks Code Example                                *
 **********************************************************************/
namespace AdvanceXpert;
public abstract class Shape
{
    // Abstract method
    public abstract double Area();
}
```

```
/**********************************************************************
 * Abstract Classes Blocks Code Example                                *
 **********************************************************************/
using AdvanceXpert;

public class Circle : Shape
{
    private double radius;

    public Circle(double radius)
    {
        this.radius = radius;
    }

    // Implementing abstract method
    public override double Area()
    {
        return Math.PI * radius * radius;
    }
}
```

Interfaces

The interface defines a contract that implementing classes must adhere to. The interface contains method signatures, properties, events, and indexers, but it does not contain method implementations.

```
/********************************************************************
* Interface Classes Blocks Code Example                             *
********************************************************************/
namespace AdvanceXpert;
public interface IShape
{
   // Method signature
   double Area();
}
```

```
/********************************************************************
* Interface Classes Blocks Code Example                             *
********************************************************************/
namespace AdvanceXpert;
public class Rectangle : IShape
{
   private double width;
   private double height;

   public Rectangle(double width, double height)
   {
      this.width = width;
      this.height = height;
   }

   // Implementing interface method
   public double Area()
   {
      return width * height;
   }
}
```

Method Overriding and Virtual Methods

In this way, derived classes can provide a specific implementation of a method defined in a base class. This is enabled by virtual methods in the base class.

```
/********************************************************************
* Method Overriding and Virtual Methods Code Example                *
********************************************************************/
namespace AdvanceXpert;
public class Animal
{
   public virtual void MakeSound()
   {
      Console.WriteLine("Animal makes a sound");
   }
}
```

Access Modifiers and Class Members

It is possible for class members to be hidden or visible depending on the access modifier. Public, private, protected, internal, and protected internal are the most common access modifiers in C#. Class members include fields, properties, methods, constructors, and events.

```csharp
public class MyClass
{
    private int privateField;

    public int PublicProperty { get; set; }

    protected void ProtectedMethod() { }

    internal int InternalField;

    protected internal int ProtectedInternalField;
}
```

```csharp
/**********************************************************************
* Method Overriding and Virtual Methods Code Example                  *
**********************************************************************/
namespace AdvanceXpert;
public class Dog : Animal
{
   // Override virtual method
   public override void MakeSound()
   {
      Console.WriteLine("Dog barks");
   }
}
```

Delegates and Events

A delegate is a type-safe function pointer that references a method with a specific signature. Events let classes interact with one another.

```
/********************************************************************
*Delegates and Events Code Example                                  *
********************************************************************/
namespace AdvanceXpert;

public delegate void EventHandler(object sender, EventArgs e);

public class Button
{
   public event EventHandler Click;

   public void OnClick()
   {
      Click?.Invoke(this, EventArgs.Empty);
   }
}
```

Generics and Collections

The generic collection type allows classes and methods to work with any data type while maintaining type safety. Common generic collection types include List<T>, Dictionary<TKey, TValue>, and HashSet<T>.

```
/********************************************************************
* Generics and Collections Code Example                             *
********************************************************************/
namespace AdvanceXpert;
public class GenericList<T>
{
   private List<T> items = new List<T>();

   public void Add(T item)
   {
      items.Add(item);
   }

   public T Get(int index)
   {
      return items[index];
   }
}
```

LINQ (Language Integrated Query)

The LINQ language provides query expressions and methods for filtering, sorting, and projecting data from various data sources such as objects, databases, and XML.

```
var numbers = new List<int> { 1, 2, 3, 4, 5 };

var evenNumbers = numbers.Where(n => n % 2 == 0);
```

Lambda Expressions and LINQ

They are commonly used when filtering, sorting, and projecting operations are required. Lambda expressions are anonymous inline functions that create delegates or expression trees.

```
Func<int, bool> isEven = n => n % 2 == 0;

var evenNumbers = numbers.Where(isEven);
```

Attributes and Reflection

The attributes provide additional information about types and members, and reflection allows them to be inspected and manipulated at runtime.

```
[Serializable]

public class MyClass { }


var type = typeof(MyClass);

var attributes = type.GetCustomAttributes();
```

Wrapping Up Advanced Topics

Developing proficient C# developers requires an understanding of abstract classes, interfaces, method overriding, access modifiers, delegate, generics, LINQ, and reflection. Using these concepts, you can write flexible, maintainable, and efficient code, which forms the basis for building complex and scalable applications. Be sure to explore these topics further and apply them effectively in your projects as you continue your development journey in C#.

Chapter 14: C# 12 Features

Overview of New Features in C# 12

A number of new and exciting features have been added to C# 12 designed to improve developer productivity, code expressiveness, and performance. Let's take a closer look at some of them:

Pattern Matching Enhancements

As a result of new features such as recursive patterns, relational patterns, and switch expressions, pattern matching has become more powerful and expressive.

```csharp
 using System.Collections;

Console.WriteLine("Hello, from Ziggy Rafiq");
Console.WriteLine("This Code Example Project is for Chapter 14");


/***********************************************************
* Pattern Matching Enhancements Code Example               *
***********************************************************/

// Relational patterns
int value = 10;
string result = value switch
{
   < 0 => "Negative",
   > 0 => "Positive",
   _ => "Zero"
};


// Recursive patterns
bool IsEmpty(object obj) => obj is null || (obj is IEnumerable enumerable && !enumerable.Cast<object>().Any());
```

Record Types

Immutable types are declared using record types, which automatically generate value-based equality, immutability, and deconstruction.

```
/***********************************************************************
* Record Types Code Example                                            *
***********************************************************************/
namespace CSharp12Innovate
{
    public record Person(string FirstName, string LastName);
}

using CSharp12Innovate;
using System.Collections;

Console.WriteLine("Hello, from Ziggy Rafiq");
Console.WriteLine("This Code Example Project is for Chapter 14");


/***********************************************************************
* Pattern Matching Enhancements Code Example                           *
***********************************************************************/

//Record Types
var person1 = new Person("Lisa", "Hills");
var person2 = new Person("Lisa", "Hills");

// The result is true
Console.WriteLine(person1 == person2);
```

Switch Expressions

A number of new features have been added to switch expressions, such as arm expressions and property patterns, to make code more concise and expressive.

```
using CSharp12Innovate;
using System.Collections;

Console.WriteLine("Hello, from Ziggy Rafiq");
Console.WriteLine("This Code Example Project is for Chapter 14");


/***********************************************************************
* Pattern Matching Enhancements Code Example                           *
***********************************************************************/

string operation = "+";
string result2 = operation switch
{
    "+" => "Addition",
    "-" => "Subtraction",
    _ => "Unknown"
};
Console.WriteLine($"The Result2 is {result2}");
```

Examples and Practical Usage
We'll take a look at some practical applications for these new features:

Simplifying Code with Records
When dealing with immutable data types, records can simplify code:

var person = new Person("Alice", "Smith");

var updatedPerson = person with { LastName = "Johnson" };

Expressive Switch Expressions
Complex conditional logic can be expressed concisely with switch expressions:

string result = operation switch

{

   "+" => "Addition",

   "-" => "Subtraction",

   _ => "Unknown"

};

Best Practices for Adoption
A few things to consider when adopting new features from C# 12:

- Start by understanding how the new features will benefit you.
- Consider the suitability of each feature according to your specific requirements.
- Consider existing code and compatibility with older versions of C#.
- Maintain backward compatibility while introducing new features gradually.

Future Trends and Advancements
With C# continuing to evolve, we can expect further improvements in performance, language expressiveness, and tooling support. Utilizing the full potential of the language requires staying up to date with the latest developments and advancements in the C# ecosystem. To stay on top of C# development, keep an eye out for official announcements, community discussions, and industry trends.

Chapter 15: Best Practices and Tips

Coding Standards and Conventions
Keeping codebases consistent and readable is crucial in C#. Here are a few coding standards and conventions:

Naming Conventions

```csharp
// PascalCase for class names
public class MyClass
{
    // camelCase for method names
    public void MyMethod()
    {
        // camelCase for variables
        int myVariable = 42;
    }
}
```

Formatting Rules

```csharp
// Consistent indentation
if (condition)
{
    // Code block
}
else
{
    // Another code block
}
```

Commenting Practices
// Single-line comment

/*

 * Multi-line comment

 */

Performance Optimization Techniques
Several techniques can be used to improve the performance of C# code. These include:

Algorithm Optimization
// Optimize algorithms for better performance

Data Caching
// Cache frequently accessed data

Asynchronous Programming
// Use async/await for non-blocking operations

Debugging and Troubleshooting Strategies

A developer's essential skill is debugging and troubleshooting C# code. Here's how you can do it:

Visual Studio Debugging Tools
// Utilize breakpoints, watch windows, and stack traces

Diagnosing Common Issues
// Identify null reference exceptions, logical errors, and performance bottlenecks

Writing Clean and Maintainable Code
Keeping your code clean and maintainable will make it easier to modify, extend, and understand. Follow these guidelines:

Code Readability
// Write clear and self-explanatory code

Modularity
// Encapsulate functionality into reusable modules

Documentation and Commenting
Use comments and documentation comments effectively to understand your code's purpose and usage.

Comments for Clarity
// Comment explaining the purpose of the code

XML Documentation
/// <summary>

/// Method summary

/// </summary>

/// <param name="param">Parameter description</param>

/// <returns>Return value description</returns>

Continuous Improvement and Learning
C# developers should always continue to improve and learn in order to be effective. Staying up-to-date with the latest trends, best practices, and advancements will enable you to become a more effective developer.

Stay Updated
Through various channels, stay up-to-date with the latest C# and software development developments:

Online Communities
Develop your skills by participating in discussions, seeking advice, and sharing your knowledge in developer communities such as Stack Overflow, Reddit, and GitHub.

Conferences and Workshops
Invest the time in attending conferences, workshops, and seminars, both online and offline. These events will provide you with valuable insights, networking opportunities, and exposure to new technologies and methodologies.

Additional Resources
Explore a wide range of C# and software development resources such as books, tutorials, online courses, and blogs. Develop your knowledge and skills by engaging in a variety of learning activities.

Embrace Lifelong Learning
As the software development industry continues to evolve, embracing a growth mindset and seeking new opportunities will allow you to stay ahead of the competition.

Apply What You Learn
By incorporating newly acquired knowledge into your projects, experimenting with different approaches, and striving for better code quality, you'll gain value from learning new concepts and techniques.

Share and Collaborate

Engage in open-source projects, participate in code reviews, and mentor others to foster a culture of knowledge sharing and collaboration in the developer community.

It takes dedication, continuous learning, and a commitment to excellence to master C# and excel in software development. You can make significant contributions to the world of technology by following best practices, staying abreast of industry trends, and embracing a mindset of continuous improvement as a C# developer. Continue to code, keep learning, and have fun on your journey to becoming an exceptional C# developer!

Chapter 16: Closing Off

Summary of Key Concepts

The following is a recap of the key concepts covered in each chapter of this comprehensive guide:

Introduction to C# Programming

The basics of C# programming languages, including variables, data types, control structures, and input/output operations, were introduced.

Understanding C# Syntax

The purpose of this chapter was to provide insight into the syntax of the C# programming language, including statements, expressions, operators, and namespaces.

Working with Data Types and Variables

C# Data Types and Variables: You explored the various data types in C# and learned how to declare variables, perform type conversions, and work with constants.

Operators and Expressions

Expressions and Operators: This chapter covers arithmetic, relational, logical, and bitwise operators, as well as precedence and associativity rules.

Control Flow and Decision Making

Branching and control flow mechanisms were discussed in conjunction with conditional statements and looping structures in C#.

Arrays and Collections

This chapter introduces arrays, lists, dictionaries, and other types of collections in C#, along with how to manipulate, sort, and iterate them.

Methods and Functions

Declaring and calling methods, passing parameters, returning values, handling method overloading, and best practices for working with methods and functions were discussed.

Object-Oriented Programming (OOP) Basics

This chapter discussed classes, objects, encapsulation, inheritance, polymorphism, constructors, destructors, and access modifiers.

Exception Handling

A chapter on exception handling in C# discussed try-catch blocks, throwing and catching exceptions, try-catch-finally blocks, custom exception classes, and best practices.

File I/O and Serialization

The course covered file input/output operations, working with streams and readers/writers, object serialization and deserialization, handling exceptions in file I/O operations, and best practices for file I/O and serialization.

Introduction to Asynchronous Programming
In this chapter, we have discussed asynchronous and synchronous operations, async and await keywords, handling asynchronous exceptions, asynchronous programming patterns, and best practices for asynchronous programming.

Working with Databases
The chapter covered connecting to databases using ADO.NET, running SQL queries and commands, working with datasets, handling exceptions, and working with database best practices.

Introduction to Web Development with C#
This chapter covers ASP.NET and web development frameworks, building simple web applications, MVC architecture, creating a simple MVC application, and best practices for web development.

C# 12 Features
You explored the features introduced in C# 12, including language enhancements, syntax changes, and their practical application.

Best Practices and Tips
The chapter discussed coding standards, performance optimization techniques, debugging and troubleshooting strategies, writing clean and maintainable code, documentation and commenting, and continuous improvement.

Further Resources for Continued Learning
Here are some resources to help you on your journey to mastering C# programming:

Books
Three books can help you learn C# in depth: "C# in Depth" by Jon Skeet, "Effective C#: 50 Specific Ways to Improve Your C#" by Bill Wagner, and "Pro C# 9" by Andrew Troelsen.

Online Courses
C# courses are available online from Pluralsight, Udemy, Coursera, and Codecademy.

Tutorials and Documentation
Learn how to develop in C# and .NET with Microsoft's official tutorials.

Open-Source Projects
Contribute to open-source projects on GitHub to gain practical experience and collaborate with others.

Community Forums
Ask questions, share knowledge, and learn from others in online communities such as Stack Overflow and Reddit.

Final Thoughts

It requires dedication, practice, and continuous learning to master the C# programming language. Remember to apply best practices, stay on top of the latest developments, and embrace a lifelong learning mindset as you explore and experiment with C#. It is possible to become proficient in C# programming with persistence and determination.

www.ingramcontent.com/pod-product-compliance
Lightning Source LLC
Chambersburg PA
CBHW062316220526
45479CB00004B/1187